Benedict XV

Courageous Prophet of Peace

by
Fr Ashley Beck

All booklets are published thanks to the generous support of the members of the Catholic Truth Society

CATHOLIC TRUTH SOCIETY
PUBLISHERS TO THE HOLY SEE

Contents

Acknowledgements

I am grateful for comments from parishioners in Beckenham following talks I have given and papers I have circulated about peace, the role of the Church in the First World War, and the observance of Remembrance Sunday. I would also like to thank Fr Owen Hardwicke, Deacon Michael Phelan, Pat Gaffney, and Doreen Jansen for their comments and support.

Much of this booklet was written in quiet moments during a school journey trip organised by St Mary's Primary School, Beckenham, to Devon in May 2007. I would like to dedicate this to the staff and pupils of the school in the hope that our children will never have to fight in war.

A man of peace

In August 1917 took place one of the least noticed events of the First World War: the publication of the 'Peace Note' of Pope Benedict XV in an effort to bring about a negotiated end to the war, which has remained one of the most horrific conflicts in human history. This anniversary is a good point to evaluate that Pope's actions during the war and the striking originality and influence of his teaching about peace and war – although much of this was ignored at the time, even by bishops and priests, it has helped to develop Christian teaching about war and peace in a way that could not have been foreseen at the time. This underrated successor of St Peter and Vicar of Christ was thus a prophet ahead of his time.

I am concentrating on Benedict's role in the war – which occupied most of his short pontificate of seven and a half years - and his teaching about peace, rather than other subjects such as his place within Italian political life or the 'modernist crisis'; nor is there any coverage of one of the most longstanding achievements of his reign, the publication of a unified Code of Canon Law in 1917. John Pollard's outstanding biography[1], which is based on important primary sources (including diaries of Benedict's friend Baron Carlo Monti which were only published in 1997) provides a comprehensive account of his life.

Attitudes to war

In recent years the opposition of the Catholic Church to the war in Iraq, and the strengthening of Christian condemnation of nuclear weapons, have brought into sharper focus the teachings and diplomatic activity of Benedict XV during the horrors of ninety years ago. At the same time many of the ways in which our society commemorates those who have died in warfare have their roots in that terrible conflict, which has also earned a special place in cultural and literary life. It is clear that both the conflict itself, because of the sheer scale of the loss of life on all sides and the futility of so many of the military engagements, has helped to change attitudes towards war, in spite of the conflict of 1939-1945; for Christians, and for Catholics in particular, this shift has been even more marked because of what Pope Benedict said and did: so we should know more about him and do more to honour his memory and heed his teachings. As we shall see, the extent to which Benedict's prophetic ministry was undermined by his flock – and in particular by the bishops in communion with him – is an essential part of how we should look on his ministry with hindsight and with sorrow. In an age when we can take it for granted that the bishops of the Catholic Church will be loyal to the Holy Father we find this deeply shocking: it shows how poisonous unthinking patriotism can be.

The statue of Benedict XV in Istanbul.

The authors of a major American Catholic critique of the Iraq War[2] dedicated their collection of essays to the present Holy Father, but also honoured the memory of his predecessor Benedict XV[3] and quoted the inscription on his statue outside the Papal Nunciature in Istanbul: this was erected in 1921 partly in recognition of how the Pope had helped so many people suffering in Turkey:

'To the great Pope of the world's tragic hour,
Benedict XV, benefactor of the people,
without discrimination or nationality or religion:
a token of gratitude from the orient.'

It is striking that this statue to the 'Pope of peace' was erected in a Muslim country when so-called 'Christian' Europe was busy erecting statues of the soldiers and politicians who had directed and prolonged the carnage of the war. In November and December 2006 Pope Benedict XVI, who recalled his predecessor when he took the name 'Benedict' shortly after his election in 2005[4], made a very important pilgrimage to Turkey as a messenger of peace and reconciliation. He celebrated his concluding Mass in the Catholic cathedral of the Holy Spirit outside which the statue stands, and released a dove outside as symbol of peace and reconciliation. The City Council of Istanbul had the statue cleaned in advance of the Holy Father's visit. If we are serious about that message we need to take to our hearts the teachings of his predecessor: his message of peace and reconciliation is needed just as much today.

'James of the Church' - priest and bishop

Early life and ministry

Giacomo della Chiesa – 'James of the Church' – was born in Genoa in northern Italy on 21st November 1854. He was from an old noble family – his father was a *Marchese* (Marquis) – which had been important in the days of the medieval Genoese republic. In spite of this the family was not wealthy by the middle of the 19th century – indeed, Della Chiesa's early studies after university were financed by a wealthy cousin. Giacomo was born prematurely, and this was the reason for a certain amount of frailty in his health and a limp which marked his whole life. After graduating from the Royal University of Genoa he went to study for the priesthood in Rome, gaining doctorates in theology and canon law, and then entered the famous Academy of Noble Ecclesiastics, the elite training ground for papal diplomats. Della Chiesa had developed from an early age a vocation to priesthood, something counter-cultural in a city like Genoa, at that time known to be anti-clerical.

To understand the future Pope we need to have some awareness of what life was like for loyal Catholics in the years following the proclamation of the Kingdom of Italy in 1870. For Blessed Pius IX and the vast majority of committed Catholics in Italy conflict and antagonism between the State and the Church were inevitable, for two principal reasons: first, the military conquest of the papal states in the 1860s and the virtual ending of the 'temporal power' of the papacy (which had always been seen as essential for the Church's independence), making the Pope a prisoner from 1870 in the Vatican; and second, the secularism and anticlericalism of the Kingdom of Sardinia and the new Kingdom of Italy, dominated by Freemasonry, leading to the exclusion of the Church from major areas of public life, particularly education. From a Catholic point of view, this marginalisation and relegation of religion to a private sphere was (and is) an attack on the faith and a denial of religious freedom: when God is pushed out of the visible life of the State, terrible consequences follow, as Della Chiesa pointed out in his attacks on the First World War many years later.

Diplomatic service

As a young priest entering the diplomatic service of the Holy See, the young Della Chiesa attracted the attention of the one of the papacy's 'rising stars', Monsignor (later Cardinal) Mariano Rampolla del Tindaro. He had him appointed to a professorship at the academy and an important post in the Vatican Secretariat of State, and in 1883 when Rampolla was made nuncio to Spain Della

Chiesa accompanied him to Madrid as secretary of the Nunciature. Many of the political tensions affecting the Church in Spain were similar to those in Italy. Four years later he returned to Rome when his mentor became Pope Leo XIII's Secretary of State and a cardinal. Leo and Rampolla greatly increased the Holy See's involvement in world politics, and as Rampolla's most important subordinate Della Chiesa was closely engaged with this and built up considerable knowledge and experience. It was also the era of *Rerum Novarum*, the Pope's great encyclical of 1891 on social issues which firmly placed the Catholic Church on the side of the workers in industrialised countries, campaigning for their rights and decent working conditions. A few years later Della Chiesa wrote to a friend: 'The Holy See wishes to see the bosses and the rich taken down a peg or two, and does not disapprove of the talk about the rights of workers; at the same time, however, it is necessary not to forget to remind them of their duties.'[5] In all this period Della Chiesa built up a formidable reputation for solving problems and was known to have a tremendous memory for detail; he was very short and was known by the nickname *il picoletto*, 'the little one.'

Following the election in 1903 of St Pius X Cardinal Rampolla's influence suffered an eclipse, and Della Chiesa remained working in the Secretariat of State; he also helped pastorally in a Roman parish near where he lived. These were tumultuous years for the Church: within the Catholic community the modernist crisis was a dominant feature of life leading to the diplomatic rupture with France in 1905.

The diplomatic vocation and peace

There is sometimes a tendency within the Church to look cynically at the diplomatic activities of the Holy See, to question whether it is really necessary and to be disdainful of priests who are engaged with it, in spite of the large number of Popes in recent centuries who have served in this area of the Church's life. However, when we look at Giacomo Della Chiesa's life it is worth reflecting on its importance in two fundamental respects: first, the need to preserve and extend the independent influence of the Church in the world, and second, the preservation of peace and avoidance of war. Of course, for much of the Church's history the first was far more important than the second; in the late 19th and early 20th centuries the unresolved 'Roman Question', the tortuous relationship between the Church and the Kingdom of Italy dominated the whole of the Church's diplomatic activity.

And yet ironically (and it did not seem so at the time) the freeing of the Church of 'temporal power' would have had the effect of enhancing, not diminishing, its independence and making it a more effective voice for peace in the world: this only gradually became clear.

Diplomacy is about negotiation, quiet 'behind the scenes' activity, not grand public gestures; it also exists to enable states to avoid going to war to settle disputes. The true diplomat will always insist on negotiating long after the politician or the soldier has opted for the use of force – war is always a defeat for diplomacy. In our own time, when so often we are told that this or that country or faction cannot be a partner in negotiation except under conditions (or perhaps not at all), the conscientious diplomat will always be questioning this, always gently saying, 'Never say never!' If we look at colonial and post-colonial conflicts of the last century, negotiations have always had to take place in the end between those who had earlier refused to sit at the same table: in this respect the diplomat, searching for common ground and constantly urging compromise, is the pioneer of peace and reconciliation. Pope Benedict XV's urgings in the First World War were the fruits of the 'science of peace' (to use the phrase coined many years later by John Paul II) which he learned in his long years in the Secretariat of State.

Archbishop of Bologna

In December 1907 Monsignor Della Chiesa was appointed Archbishop of Bologna. While this is one of the most important Italian sees, the appointment is usually seen as sign that Della Chiesa's influence had declined in the Vatican,[6] but it gave him great scope for his pastoral and administrative gifts – he also needed to be diplomatic, as Bologna and the region of Emilia-Romagna at the time was dominated by very anti-clerical forces. The city and the region were also centres of gastronomic excellence and prosperous, as they are today.

Archbishop Della Chiesa began his ministry with a letter stressing the teaching office of the bishop, and this remained a theme of his episcopacy; he also reorganised the administration of the diocese and conducted a thorough visitation of the parishes of the archdiocese: this was demanding as many were in remote mountain villages, many of which could only be reached by horseback: there are copious records of these visitations.[7] As far as ecclesiastical controversies were concerned, and particularly the wish of the Holy See to suppress modernism, the archbishop combined unimpeachable orthodoxy and loyalty to the pope with a desire to maintain unity and show respect to individuals. In his political disputes with some of those in power in Emilia-Bologna, Della Chiesa was adamant that political extremism was intent on drawing people away from the practice of the Catholic faith.

Cardinal

After a rather long gap of seven years Della Chiesa was created a cardinal in May 1914. Since Bologna is a very senior Italian see this delay caused considerable ill-feeling in the city and can only be explained in terms of some continuing disfavour in Rome. We can see clearly that in his seven years in Bologna Della Chiesa built on his formidable diplomatic and administrative experience and showed great pastoral and teaching gifts.

The First World War and the new Pope

Death of St Pius X and the conclave

Europe was plunged into the First World War in the closing days of July 1914, a few weeks after the assassination of the Archduke Francis Ferdinand and his wife in Sarajevo. At this terrible turning point in European history, the Church was soon to be left leaderless as St Pius X died on 21st August, the day Brussels fell – some said of a broken heart, caused by the outbreak of a war he had long predicted; he pleaded for it to stop on 2nd August. Diplomatically the Holy See was so weak - very few of the belligerent countries even had diplomatic representatives at the Vatican – and there had been little Pius and his Secretary of State, Cardinal Merry del Val, could do to prevent the outbreak of war. The cardinals, including the newly elevated Archbishop of Bologna, assembled hurriedly[8] to elect a successor. The shadow of the war, and the terrible things being done in the war, hung over the cardinals. When Cardinal Hartmann, Archbishop of Cologne, met the Archbishop of Brussells-Malines, Cardinal Mercier (later famous for his theological conversation with High Church Anglicans) he said 'I hope that we shall not speak of war', to which his Belgian colleague replied, 'And I hope that we shall not speak of peace.' This depressing exchange[9], reflecting the early brutalities carried out by German soldiers in Belgium and the invasion of the country in contravention of international treaty obligations, illustrates the how far the war would sunder the unity of the Catholic Church. However, it is likely that ecclesiastical politics were more important than the war in determining the result of the conclave when Della Chiesa was elected pope on 3 September. He was seen as a 'moderate' in terms of the polarised factions and their favoured candidates among the Italian cardinals (the war made it even less likely than it might have been for a non-Italian to be elected).

Elected Pope

Della Chiesa caused some surprise by choosing the name Benedict. Like his own successor, the present Benedict XVI, he chose the name partly because of St Benedict, the founder of western monasticism - he and his order had '*Pax*', 'peace' as its motto; it may also be because of Benedict XIV (1740-58), the last Archbishop of Bologna to be elected pope. He reacted with great humanity, and some humour, to the election. When it became clear that even the smallest white papal cassock that had been prepared was too big for him, he said to the tailor, 'My dear, had you forgotten me?' and he also wept as the bells of Rome started ringing.[10] Benedict's humanity and gentleness (although he was also at times short-tempered) are an important backdrop for his theology of reconciliation and peace. Out of respect for those suffering already in the war, he decided to scale down his coronation to a smaller ceremony in the Sistine Chapel rather than St Peter's. Since the last papal coronation was in the 1960s we need to remind ourselves of some of the ritual which used to mark the beginning of the ministry of the successor of Peter: in Benedict's case some of it was particularly apt. First, the point in the ceremony when a plate was put in front of the pope with some flax soaked in oil was ignited. Onlookers saw a bright flare of light and then some greasy smoke, as a prelate chanted before the pope, '*Sancte pater, sic transit gloria mundi!*' ('Holy Father, thus passes the glory of the world!') While one biographer[11] sees this as a symbol of Benedict's short reign and the extent to which it has been forgotten, it is a far clearer symbol of the horror of the First World War and how much of the 'glory of the world' went up in flames and smoke. A clear symbol of the loyalty which the Holy See is entitled to expect, above patriotism, is the exhortation said as the papal tiara was placed on Benedict's head: 'Receive this tiara adorned with three crowns, and know thyself to be he Ruler of the World, the Father of Princes and Kings, the earthly Vicar of Jesus Christ our Saviour.'

What was clear very quickly was that Benedict was his 'own man'.- he appointed as his Secretary of State (replacing Merry Del Val) his old friend and colleague Pietro Gasparri, much more favourable to the French than the previous regime.

Call for peace and first encyclical

Five days after his election, on 8 September, Benedict issued his first plea (in the Apostolic exhortation, *Ubi Primum*) for the end of the war. He called on belligerent nations 'to leave nothing undone to hasten the end of this calamity' and asks that 'the rulers of the peoples *be satisfied with the ruin already wrought*.'[12] Although many in the Vatican (and the rest of Europe) expected the war to be over by Christmas, we see the beginnings of Benedict's urgent tone, and strong sense in which he saw the leaders of the warring powers as being subject to God's judgement. This sense of urgency can also be seen in his first encyclical letter, *Ad Beatissimi*, significantly published on All Saints Day, one of the greatest feast days of the Christian year which points Catholics towards life in heaven with God, and the day before All Souls Day, the 'Day of the Dead', an observance which had more poignancy in Europe in 1914 because of the thousands already slaughtered since August. Expectations that the war would be over by Christmas were evaporating as the stalemate on the Western front had now become established with the line of trenches from the sea to the Ardennes, following the battles of the Marne and 'First' Ypres. The position in the East was similarly undecided, and no-one hoping for an early end to the war would have taken heart from Turkey's entry into the war in October. The pope's letter is largely made up of an analysis of the causes of the war. To begin with, it is about lack of mutual love, of charity – 'the absence in relations between men of mutual love with their fellow men…race hatred[13] has reached its climax...'. Another cause, which draws on his pastoral experience in Italy, is lack of respect for authority and the sidelining of God: '…contempt for authority, the injustice in the relations between classes and the attainment of material goods made into the sole object of human activity and the unrestrained striving after independence.' He also makes the plea he was to repeat many times: 'Surely there are other ways and means whereby violated rights can be rectified?' All these evils are countered by Jesus in his Sermon on the Mount. For the pope to begin his pontificate with an encyclical devoted to the war was the clearest possible sign that striving for an end to the carnage would be at the heart of his ministry. We can see, nevertheless, that his utterances were apt to draw criticism and cause offence from the very beginning: apparently the French took offence at his use of the term *fraternité* in the encyclical.[14]

Christmas message

A book and a celebrated feature film[15] marked the ninetieth anniversary of the unofficial Christmas truce observed by some soldiers on the western front in 1914. Benedict tried hard to get such a truce officially observed, the ancient idea of the *Treuga Dei*. It seems as if the French were the most vigorous opponents of the pope's call[16]. Benedict issued a trenchant message on Christmas Eve, full of passion: 'It seems as if the Divine Spirit says to us in the prophet: *Clamas, ne cesses* – "Cry out, cease not!" Ah! May the fratricidal weapons fall to the ground, may they fall at last, stained as they already are by too much blood… Cry out, and do not stop, and We praise the pastors and single individuals who have determined to promote or multiply public or private prayer *to do sweet violence to the Most Sacred Heart of Jesus* to obtain that an end may come to the terrible scourge which now grips and throttles such a great part of the world.'

Benedict's work for peace in early 1915

The beginning of 1915 was marked by growing pressure on the Holy See from the Entente nations, particularly France and Britain, to condemn atrocities committed by the Germans in occupied Belgium. There had been strong feelings on both sides from the beginning of the war that the pope was not as neutral in the conflict as he claimed to be. On the one hand, his association earlier in his life with Cardinal Rampolla led the Austrians and Germans to view him as pro-French, and their cardinals voted against him in the conclave; although Austria-Hungary had a close historical relationship with the Holy See (and the Emperor was a very devout Catholic), which feared for its survival, the dominant power in Germany was Protestant Prussia, which had led a campaign against Catholics under Bismarck, the *Kulturkampf*, in the 1880s, although Bavaria and much of western Germany was staunchly Catholic. On the other, the still bad relationship with France, dominated by anticlerical and Masonic politicians and newspapers, meant that almost anything the Holy See did would be subject to criticism, so that Benedict was openly referred as *le pape Boche* and attacked by politicians such as Leon Blum; Britain was a country with a deep history of anti-Catholicism (although things were improving by this time) – and this was true of the Prime Minister, H. H. Asquith and the Conservative leader Arthur Balfour.[17] Russia was strongly Eastern Orthodox (subjugating many Catholics in Poland and Lithuania) and suspicious of the Catholic Church. While Belgium, whose neutrality had been violated by Germany, bringing Britain into the war, was a strongly Catholic country, the Entente powers had very limited or non-existent diplomatic links with the Vatican compared to Austria-Hungary and Germany (which had a second delegation there for Bavaria).[18]

Impartiality

The invasion of Belgium, deportations and executions of civilians, the ill-treatment accorded to the Primate, Cardinal Desiré Mercier, the sack of Louvain and the burning of the university library all caused outrage among Catholics all over the world. In Britain, the Church organised support for hundreds of Belgian refugees coming into the country, and this helped to rally Catholics behind the war effort. The Holy See reacted with caution,[19] but the pope made it clear that 'We do proclaim it without modification, condemning openly every injustice by whatever side it is committed.'[20] - and this even-handedness was followed by a specific criticism of the violation of Belgian neutrality[21] which led to sustained attacks on Benedict in the German press and his being labelled *Der Französische Papst*.

Not for the last time, combatant countries could not understand that the international character of the Catholic Church cuts across national rivalries and conditions how the Church responds to specific incidents. It meant that over another issue relating to international law, the Holy See was careful to be critical of both sides. As the war intensified Benedict and Cardinal Gasparri denounced both the Entente naval blockade of the Central Powers (which in the end played a major role in bringing the war to an end finally in 1918) and the corresponding German

U-Boat campaign against merchant shipping of both combatant and neutral powers, which did so much to bring the USA into the war in 1917. It is likely that the pope was right to see both actions as violations of international law[22] and as 1915 progressed Benedict criticised the submarine campaign and in the course of 1916 was successful in moderating the German actions, leading to assurances that passenger liners would not be attacked. His anxiety was partly that outrage at the loss of life was increasing the likelihood that the USA would join the war (which is partly what happened), although he was also strongly critical of the supply of arms to the British and the French by the Americans which he viewed as illegal[23] - in an interview in a New York newspaper in April 1915 he called on the United States to enforce an arms embargo against both sides[24].

Italy and the War

However, in the first months of 1915 the pope's priority was to try and keep Italy out of the war. He did this by trying to persuade Austria to cede its Italian-speaking provinces of Trieste and Trento – increasingly the Italian government saw 'regaining' these territories, the 'unredeemed lands', as the last remaining act in the unification of the country. These efforts were unsuccessful. The tide of warlike opinion in Italy grew increasingly strong as the government also saw a nationalistic war as a good way of distracting people from increasingly serious domestic problems, in spite of a thirty-five year old treaty of friendship with Austria-Hungary and Germany, which had created the so called 'Triple Alliance'. It is also arguable that other influences were at work, since the foreign minister Sonnino was one of the most anti-clerical ministers to have held office in the Kingdom of Italy: Benedict himself certainly saw the hand of Freemasonry in the moves towards the country entering the war. Many masons in public life would have seen themselves as natural allies of the French Third Republic, in which they were also strong, over and against the Catholic Habsburg Empire; a Masonic memorandum has come to light from this period calling for a society 'without altars and without thrones.'[25] The relationship between the kingdom and the Vatican was certainly not absent from the government's calculations: in the secret article 15 of the Treaty of London in which Italy agreed to enter the war (which was only made public two years later after the Russian Revolution, following false denials by the Italian ministers that it existed), it was laid down that 'France, Great Britain and Russia shall support any such opposition as Italy shall make to any proposal in the direction of introducing a representative of the Holy See in any peace negotiations or negotiations for the settlement of questions raised by the war.'

Reasons

There were numerous reasons why Benedict was opposed to Italy entering the conflict. First, and most important, any widening of the conflict would increase the bloodletting (and indeed, he had family members living in areas not far from what became the front line). Second, the actions could never be held to fulfil the 'Just War' criteria: Italy was simply after territory. Third, he feared that any defeat in the war would further destabilise society and lead to revolution; and finally he knew that it would make the operation of papal diplomacy immeasurably more difficult. This was certainly the case, as ambassadors to the Holy See from the Central powers had to decamp to neutral Switzerland from Rome. The fact that the Vatican was known to be opposed to the war increased hostility to the pope from the press and politicians after Italy joined the war on 24th May 1915 – he was eventually dubbed *Maledetto XV* ('Accursed'). In spite of all this, most Italian Catholics rallied to the flag – the young Angelo Roncalli, the future Pope John XXIII, served as a medical orderly[26] (priests were not exempt from military service). There were many practical impediments that the Holy See now faced: many staff members were called up, newspapers and journals were censored (*L'Osservatore Romano* and *La Civiltà Cattolica*) and many visitors to the pope were subjected to surveillance. Benedict would not allow chaplains in uniform to enter the Vatican.

As Benedict had foreseen, Italy fared badly in the war. Today if you go to any Italian village and look at the war memorial, you will see far more names inscribed for the First than for the Second World War – the loss of life was horrendous. Benedict tried to prevent the bombardment of Italian towns by the Austrians, which caused outrage; the terrible defeat at the Battle of Caporetto in 1917, accompanied by the brutality towards his own soldiers of General Cadorna, restored the pope's popularity among ordinary soldiers because of his opposition to the conflict[27]. The defeat was so bad that the Italian government for a short time put out feelers through the Vatican aimed at negotiating a separate peace with Austria-Hungary.[28]

One year into the war

On the first anniversary of the war, 28th July, Benedict issued an Apostolic Exhortation 'To the Belligerent Peoples, and their Rulers', *Allorchè Fummo*, and from this time the Holy See was much more active diplomatically to end the war. Benedict was forthright in his condemnation of the conflict:

'In the holy name of God, in the name of our heavenly Father and Lord, by the precious Blood of Jesus, the price of man's redemption, we adjure you, whom Divine

Providence has placed in authority over the nations now at war, to put a final end to this horrible butchery which has been disgracing Europe for a whole year, It is the blood of brothers that is being poured out on land and sea. The most beautiful regions of Europe, the garden of the world, are strewn with corpses and with ruin. Where but a short time ago there flourished the industry of manufactures and the fruitful labours of the fields, the guns now thunder fearfully and in their destructive fury they spare neither village or city, but spread havoc and death everywhere. You bear the dread responsibility of peace and war in the sight of God and man; listen to the voice of a father, who is the vicar of the Eternal and Supreme Judge, to whom you will have to give an account of your public undertakings as well as your private actions. The abundant wealth with which God the Creator has enriched the lands that you rule enables you to continue the struggle, but at what cost? Let the thousands of young lives extinguished every day make answer; the ruins of so many towns and villages, of so many monuments raised by the piety and genius of your forefathers. And the bitter tears shed in secret at home, or at the foot of altars where the suppliants pray – do not these repeat that the price of the long protracted struggle is great, too great? Nor let it be said that this vast conflict cannot be settled without the violence of arms... Abandon the mutual threat of destruction. Remember, nations do not die; humiliated and oppressed, they bear the weight of the yoke imposed upon them, preparing themselves for their come-back and transmitting from one generation to the next a sad legacy of hatred and vendetta. Why not from this moment consider with a serene conscience the rights and just aspirations of peoples? Why not commence in good will an exchange, direct or indirect, of views with a purpose of keeping in mind as far as possible those rights and those aspirations and thus put an end to this conflict, as has happened in other circumstances? Blessed be he who first raises the olive branch of peace and extends his right hand to the enemy offering reasonable conditions for peace. The equilibrium of the world and prosperity and secure tranquillity of nations rest on mutual benevolence and the respect of the rights of and dignity of others, rather than on a multitude of armies and a formidable ring of fortresses.'[29]

Brokering peace

In 1915 Benedict received a number of delegations and international requests from groups seeking his help in the cause of peace – the Dutch Catholic State party, the American women peace activists, Jane Adams and Alice Hamilton Bach, and a number of Jewish groups alarmed at the ill treatment of Jews by the Russians.[30] At the time of the anniversary letter, the Vatican was involved in an attempt to broker a peace between Germany and her western adversaries. Benedict attempted to forward an offer to restore Belgium and set up negotiations about Alsace-Lorraine; Cardinal Mercier refused to pass the offer on to his government in exile, and it was also rejected by the French – and criticised by the head of the *Institute Catholique de France*.[31]

This was the last major initiative from the Holy See for two years; in the intervening time Benedict continued to condemn the war in public and engage in humanitarian relief and bolstering up a 'spirituality of peace', both of which we will examine below. In his Christmas message for 1915 he wrote that the world had become a 'hospital and a charnel house', and in March 1916 he referred to the 'suicide of Europe'; in July of that year he described war as 'the darkest tragedy of human hatred and human madness', and in September he told the bishops of Germany that he was 'supremely bound in conscience to counsel, suggest, inculcate nothing else but peace'; he was determined to support the cause of 'mankind rather than men' and would 'continue by every means...to alleviate, at least in part, the awful accumulation of miseries which are the sad consequences of the war.' [32]

At the end of 1916, wearied by over two years of futile conflict, one side in the war took an initiative of exploring a negotiated peace. While Germany had effectively knocked Romania out of the war, the Austrians had suffered a major defeat earlier in the year at the hands of the Russians, and in November the death of the Emperor Francis Joseph changed the attitude to the war of the Habsburg monarchy: his nephew the Emperor Blessed Charles was anxious to find a negotiated end to the war.[33] Germany in December passed different notes to the USA and the Vatican; the latter echoed much of the pope's language in earlier appeals but contained little in the way of substantial proposals. This was the main reason why Benedict and Gasparri were unenthusiastic about the German note, which was rejected by the Entente powers, leading to a resumption of unrestricted submarine warfare.[34]

Benedict and the USA

Just as in 1915 Benedict had striven unsuccessfully to stop Italy from joining the conflict, so two years later he made the same efforts with regard to the USA, and similarly failed. After the publication of the German peace note, President Woodrow Wilson made an appeal for peace, also drawing on the pope's language.[35] The final *casus belli* was the bizarre Zimmermann telegram involving German efforts to encourage Mexico to invade the USA and gain territory, but Germany's submarine warfare had soured the relationship between the two countries for some time, in spite of Benedict's efforts to moderate it. The Holy See was surprised by the eventual declaration of war in April 1917, having thought that

Irish, German and Jewish elements in American society would keep the country neutral; it is certainly hard to see consistency in Wilson's policy.[36] While for the Entente it was America's entry into the war which guaranteed eventual victory, as was true in the Second World War, for Benedict it would merely prolong the conflict.

The Peace Note of 1917

Benedict's most important initiative in the war was the Peace Note of the summer of 1917 and to this we now turn.

The context for the note

Even more than the previous winter, it seemed as if in the summer of 1917 the combatant nations were weary of the slaughter. There had been some tentative feelers given out between Britain and Austria-Hungary in Switzerland earlier in the year[37] and come contacts too between the Habsburgs and the French. Benedict had always warned of revolution and social collapse as a result of war, and the revolution in Russia (which would by the end of year remove her from the conflict) was a vivid illustration of that. The serious mutinies in the French front line in the spring of the year showed that soldiers had their limits, and there were tentative meetings of Catholic and Socialist politicians in Switzerland and Sweden. Above all, in Germany the Catholic politician Matthias Erzberger persuaded the Reichstag to pass a 'peace resolution' – he was not a long-standing opponent of the war, but one who was respected by the government who had run Germany's intelligence and propaganda operations earlier in the war.

Benedict and Gasparri rightly perceived that any initiative would only succeed if Germany was prepared to make concessions, since only the Central Powers were occupying enemy territory, especially Belgium. In May Benedict sent Mgr Eugenio Pacelli (the future Pope Pius XII) as nuncio to Bavaria (and effectively to the whole of Germany) who had meetings with the Chancellor, Bethman-Hollweg and the Kaiser – these established specific issues on the basis of which Germany would be prepared to negotiate peace – including the limitation of armaments, the setting up of international courts, negotiations about Alsace-Lorraine and, above all, the restoration of the independence of Belgium.

What the Note said

Benedict's Peace Note of 1st August was sent to the leaders of the belligerent states on the 15th, the feast of the Assumption. It is sometimes known by its opening words in French, *Dès le début*: 'Since the beginning of our pontificate, in the midst of the horrors of the terrible war which has burst upon Europe, we have considered three things among others: to maintain an absolute impartiality towards all belligerents, as becomes him who is the common father, and who loves all his children with an equal affection; to endeavour continually to do the utmost good to all without distinctions of persons, nationality or religion, in accordance not only with the universal law of charity, but also with the supreme spiritual duty laid upon us by Christ; and finally, as is demanded by our pacific mission, to omit nothing, as far as is in our power lies, to contribute to hasten the end of this calamity by trying to bring the peoples and their leaders to more moderate resolutions in the discussion of means that will secure a "just and lasting peace"'[38]

He proposed that the rule of law be restored and that the moral force of right replace the material force of arms. This needed to be done in three stages: first, fighting should be suspended; second, there should be a reduction in armaments 'according to rules and guarantees to be established to the extent necessary and sufficient for the maintenance of public order in each State'; third, there should be international arbitration 'on lines to be determined and with sanctions to be settled against any State that should refuse either to submit international questions to arbitration or to accept its awards.' He also called for occupied territories to be restored and that there should be negotiations to settle territorial disputes; the terms also provided for the free movement of peoples and common rights over the seas. Demands for reparations and indemnities should be renounced. In addition to the points already agreed in Germany, of note are the provisions for the renunciation of indemnities and the freedom and community of the seas; as can be seen Benedict set out detailed plans for negotiations in relation to a wide range of places – he referred specifically to Belgium, Poland, the Balkan states and Armenia. He ended the message:

'Lend an ear, therefore, to our prayers, accept the paternal invitation which we address to you in the name of the divine Redeemer, the Prince of Peace. Reflect on your very grave responsibility before God and before men; on your decision depend the repose and joy of unnumbered families, the lives of thousands of our young men, the happiness, in a word, of the peoples, to secure whose welfare is our absolute duty. May God inspire you with a decision in harmony with his most holy will. Heaven grant that in meriting the applause of your contemporaries you may assure to yourselves, in the sight of future generations, the noble name of peace-makers. For our part, in close communion in prayer and penitence with all the faithful souls who are longing for peace, we implore for you from the Divine Spirit enlightenment and counsel.'[39]

The failure of the initiative

The initiative failed: no-one on the Entente side showed any interest (Britain did not even show the Holy See the common courtesy of a proper reply[40]; much hostility was shown in France and Italy), and the rejection on behalf of the alliance was made by President Wilson, who had initially remarked of the pope: 'What does he want to butt in for?' We can see from the eventual response how much his attitude had changed since the previous winter: 'We cannot take the word of the present rulers of Germany as a guarantee of any thing that is to endure' – in other words, as in another place many years later, America was really interested in 'regime change'. As Peters says, 'Wilson could not endorse Benedict's plan because the prime premises of the two men differed so radically. For Benedict peace rested on a willingness to forgive. Wilson, despite his disclaimers, was motivated by an urge to punish.'[41] There were also problems on the other side: in spite of the Emperor Blessed Charles' eagerness for peace, by this stage of the war the Habsburg empire was almost entirely dependent on Germany and incapable of independent action. In Germany itself, by the time the Note was issued Bethman-Holweg had been replaced as Imperial Chancellor by Michaelis, a creature of Hindenberg and Ludendorff in the High Command, and content to do their bidding, although the Kaiser did indicate acceptance. The High Command were less interested in a negotiated peace and in giving up Belgium; with Russia weakening all the time and the U-boat campaign having been successful, they thought Germany could win quickly. There was also hostility in some circles in Germany that Benedict's initiative took place in the year when Protestants were commemorating the four hundredth anniversary of Martin Luther's Reformation.

While the initiative failed – and Benedict said that its rejection was the bitterest moment of his life – the pope in a sense had the last word as Wilson's famous 'Fourteen Points' of January 1918 was clearly inspired by many of the headings in Benedict's Note: they included a reduction in armaments, the freedom of the seas, and the removal of economic barriers.[42] Ironically too, Italy's very hostile reaction was soon overshadowed by the catastrophe of the Battle of Caporetto which almost had her rulers suing for a separate peace, and other initiatives followed in the months after August.

Disloyalty in France and England

We have seen how the Note, and earlier moves by Benedict such as his Prayer for Peace, were greeted with great hostility in the warring nations – particularly the Entente powers; some of this hostility reflected long term antagonism to the Holy See.

Ninety years later, when the Holy See, even when its policies are opposed, is treated with respect, this shocks us. But what is even more disturbing when we look at Benedict's efforts to end the First World War is the extent to which he was not supported by those who would naturally be expected to be his closest collaborators: the bishops and many other influential people in belligerent countries. After the Peace Note a preacher at the famous church of *La Madeleine* in Paris, declared, 'Holy Father, we do not want your peace.'[43] The Dominican professor at the *Institute Catholique*, P. Sertillanges, declared in the presence of the Archbishop of Paris, Cardinal Amette, 'Holy Father, for the time we are unable to listen to your words of peace. Like the apparent rebel in the gospel, we are sons who reply "No, no."'[44] In France (as in Italy), the war provided an opportunity for healing to some extent the rift between the Church and the State. The impoverishment of the Church in France since 1905, in a dispute which many felt that the Vatican had made worse than it needed to be, and the catastrophic loss of involvement in the State education, had a serious effect on the leaders of the French Church: the last thing bishops wanted was to be portrayed as unpatriotic.

In Britain

In Britain there was the same lack of support. Catholics in the Edwardian era were beginning to come 'out of the cold'; again, partly also because of troubles in Ireland, the hierarchy was anxious that Catholics should be loyal to King and country and, as we have seen, many were justly outraged at the treatment of Catholic Belgium.

But the extent of disloyalty to the Vicar of Christ is still shocking: even in the recent Iraq wars, Catholics who disagreed with the opposition of Pope John Paul II to both conflicts had the decency to keep their opinions to themselves. We can see how bad things were by simply looking at the hierarchy and the Catholic press. Cardinal Bourne, the Archbishop of Westminster, was obviously in constant contact with the Holy See, since although Britain had a minister in the Vatican there was no corresponding representative of the Holy See in London. Bourne seems to have been anxious to warn the pope not to take actions which would antagonise the British government: Benedict did not follow this advice, and the antagonism was there anyway, part of the ingrained anti-Catholicism of the British establishment. Shortly before the end of the war, in September 1918, Bourne preached these words at Our Lady of Victories, Kensington, which contrast sharply with everything Benedict said and wrote during the war: 'Be not misled. Peace is not "the greatest gift God can bestow" unless it be founded on justice. Do not be carried away by formulae such as "no indemnities, no annexations". Justice may ask for time. Peace without justice is not worth having.'[45]

The Guild of the Pope's Peace

It is instructive to look at a small organisation called *The Guild of the Pope's Peace* founded by Francis Meynell and Stanley Morison after the introduction of conscription in January 1916.[46] This existed to promote the pope's call for a negotiated peace based on arbitration, rather than the quest for total victory over Germany. It consisted of a committee of seven people, including two priests. It issued a 'Preliminary Notice' which explained that the pope had invited 'all the friends of peace in the world to help us in hastening the end of the war. It called on loyal Catholics to answer Benedict's pleas in order for them to be effective – 'The voices of many thousands must speak as one.' Somewhat remarkably (in view of what happened) the Catholic Truth Society published this notice in its monthly journal, *Catholic Book Notes*, in April 1916. The editor of the journal and secretary of the CTS, James Britten, immediately got into trouble. Cardinal Bourne asked the Duke of Norfolk to write a letter of complaint to him, indicating that the Guild had 'no authorisation of any kind'; The Bishop of Southwark, Peter Amigo, (in whose diocese the CTS offices were situated) wrote directly to the CTS committee criticising the publication of the notice in the journal[47] and later that month Britten published a written apology in *The Tablet*.

At about this time the Guild published *A Little Book of Prayers for Peace*[48] 'for the purpose of entreating God to end the scourge of war.' The Guild's critics could do little to attack this as it had a Westminster *imprimatur* (the prayers were all from existing liturgical sources, together with Benedict's own 1915 prayer) and authorisation and a blessing for the compiler from the pope himself. The book is beautifully produced and includes a number of psalms, extracts from the canon of the Mass, prayers to

Our Lady and commemorations in honour of peacemaking saints such as St Elizabeth of Portugal, the Seven Holy Founders of the Service Order, St Philp Benizi and St Michael the Archangel.

Opposition to anti-war initiatives

The Bishop of Clifton, Ambrose Burton, wrote to the press publicly condemning the Guild: 'Whatever authority be behind this stop-the-war 'Guild'...it has no sanction or countenance from us, and will receive none, as we trust, from any of our clergy and people.'[49] This was in the context of many pastoral letters and sermons from bishops calling for total victory, such as those from the Archbishop of Liverpool, two successive Bishops of Nottingham, and Bourne himself, who in a pastoral of 10th September 1916[50] declared that ultimate victory depended on God alone and that providence protected the Allies from victory by the enemy. At the same time he declared: 'The Pope has proposed that all the belligerents should come to a compromise. No! We demand the total triumph of right over wrong. We do not want a peace which will be no more than a truce or armistice between two wars. There may be in our land some people who want peace at any price, but they have no following among us. We English Catholics are fully behind our war leaders.'[51] It seems astounding to us that the chief pastor of Catholics in England and Wales, who held this position for over thirty years and is for that reason a major figure in the history of the Church in this land, should be so publicly disloyal to the Vicar of Christ; he seems to have realised that he went too far, as in subsequent statements he expressed sorrow at hostile newspaper coverage of the Peace Note.[52] In response to Bourne's statements, the Guild published a booklet which asked: 'How is it that even now, after the Pope's proposal of terms which would secure all the finer objects for which our politicians claimed to be fighting, and for which the masses of our soldiers are indeed fighting, there are many Catholics who still reject the Holy Father's mediation? Not only do they reject it, but...seeking to invent new "war aims" when they hold are in danger of realisation, many endure in silence, some even approve, the calumnies of the war press against the Holy Father.'[53]

Condemnations

Given the attitude of the bishops, the views of most of the Catholic press and some prominent lay Catholics are less surprising. *The Universe* roundly condemned the Guild in May 1916[54], backed by a journal called the *Catholic Federationist. The Catholic Times* was vociferous in calling for all-out victory[55]. *The Tablet* went so far as to reject Benedict's Peace Note[56], which did shock other organs of Catholic opinion such as the *Glasgow Observer*

– itself rather half-hearted in its respect for the pope. Similarly, President Wilson's rejection of Benedict's Note was backed by the *Catholic Times*, and only *The Universe* was mildly critical.[57] Even when bishops were attempting to defend the pope from the more vicious criticisms in the press, they did so in a way which nevertheless undermined his authority by making it clear that Catholics were free to dissent – this was explicitly done by the bishops of Salford and Northampton[58]. Prominent Catholics who were critical of the Pope's Note included Fr Bernard Vaughan and A.S Hewins; another critic of any moves towards a negotiated peace was the writer Hilaire Belloc[59] and in Rome it was also opposed by the (Catholic) British minister to the Holy See, Count de Salis, and the only British curial Cardinal, Aidan Gasquet.

Some attempts were made to rally to the pope's cause, by the Benedictine Hugh Edmund Ford[60] and two prominent Jesuits, C. C. Martindale and Charles Plater, who wrote two pamphlets, *The Pope's Peace Note* and (in response to the reactions) *Replies to the Pope's Appeal*[61]. All these authors, by careful examination of the text of the Note, showed how it had been wilfully misconstrued by those who were simply not interested in anything other than total victory. They were isolated voices: the overwhelming picture is of the leadership of the Catholic Church in Britain, clerical and lay, bending over backwards to demonstrate their loyalty to their country at war rather than to the Vicar of Christ. The irony was that this craven behaviour was not reciprocated by any respect towards the position of the Catholic Church: Catholic leaders were unhappy both about the lack of any official reply by the government to the Note, and even more outraged at the existence of the secret article 15 of the Treaty of London[62]; but their protests, and those of Catholics from all over the world, fell on deaf ears.

The teaching of Benedict XV

As is well known the Catholic Church draws on a significant tradition of teaching, known as the *Just War doctrine*, based largely on St Thomas Aquinas, to evaluate the moral licitness of military conflict. It remains very important today in many situations, and most theologians now would evaluate the conduct of most of the belligerents in World War I negatively in the light of the doctrine – partly because of the principle of proportionality, in that the terrible level of casualties outweighed the good aims which can be identified (such as defending a neutral country), and partly because the chaotic diplomacy in the weeks leading up to the beginning of the war, increasingly pushed aside by the processes of mobilisation, do not suggest that the combatants declared was as a last resort. By contrast at the time, Christian leaders in the belligerent countries thought that they were fighting in a just war, as we have seen in the statements by bishops in England and Wales; on the other side, the same sentiments can be seen, for example, in the attitude of the young Edith Stein, St Teresa Benedicta of the Cross, Patron Saint of Europe.[53] What is striking about Benedict's impassionate pleas against the war is that he does not use the Just War doctrine. His arguments are more direct, often simply dwelling on the terrible consequences of the conflict in terms of loss of life. They are not simply subjective arguments – indeed, his first encyclical, *Ad Beatissimi*, as we have seen, contains a substantial and scientific analysis of the war's causes. Perhaps one reason why so many Catholics in belligerent nations felt entitled to distance themselves from his teaching was that his approach avoided the traditional manner of analysis according to the Just War criteria and made a much simpler claim (which actually lies at the basis of the Just War doctrine) – that war is simply wrong and a moral evil.

New role for the Holy See

Benedict was the first pope to have to react to a continental or world conflict in a world of modern communications; even in previous European conflicts, such as the Napoleonic wars, the Holy See was as much one of the temporal powers involved as a spiritual authority (for much of it the pope had been a prisoner of the French); moreover modern warfare, with more devastating methods of killing people, was a new phenomenon. We can see that the development of modern warfare in the twentieth century has had the effect of driving Christian teaching to be more and more negative about war *per se* – and in this process Benedict's teaching was clearly pioneering and prophetic.

Some commentators may feel that aspects of this have not always been helpful. Controversy may always surround the role of Pope Pius XII in World War II[64], but he saw himself as fulfilling the same sort of role as Benedict, as a peacemaker, rather than one taking sides in the conflict: as nuncio in Bavaria, Mgr Eugenio Pacelli had been instrumental in the discussions leading to the Peace Note. It is far easier to justify Britain's war aims in the Second World War in terms of Christian teaching than it was in the First, but the eventual effect of the war contributed to the same process of forming a clear 'anti-war' teaching from the churches: that is why most of us are so shocked when we read of what Church leaders in Britain said and wrote during the Great War. Benedict was ahead of his time.

Long term influence

The clearest sign of his teaching's long term influence is the great encyclical of his successor Blessed John XXIII, *Pacem in Terris*, written at the very end of his life in June 1963.[65] He actually refers to the Peace Note in a footnote to section 112 (dealing with disarmament; there is also a reference to a broadcast by Pius XII), but his indebtedness to Benedict goes far deeper. Much of John's pontificate, especially in its closing period, was devoted to the cause of peace. At the end of 1962 the Cuban missile crisis had brought the world close to nuclear war and the pope played an important part in reducing the tension, and shortly afterwards he met Kruschev's daughter and her husband in the Vatican[66]. *Pacem in Terris* is John's last testament; he saw its publication as a religious act rather than a diplomatic move, signing it on Maundy Thursday at a public ceremony at which he wore a stole to give the act religious significance.

John (who, as we saw above, had been an army medical orderly in World War I) makes the same link as Benedict had between peace and religious belief, as the opening words of the letter assert: 'Peace on earth – which humanity throughout the ages has so longed for and sought after – can never be established, never guaranteed, except by the diligent observance of the divinely established order.' Benedict had also made the same connection between peace and *order*, constantly warning that total war brought the danger of social disintegration and revolution. The whole of the first section of *Pacem in Terris* reflects on peace in the light of what human society is about and the rights and responsibilities of men and women; this recalls Benedict's analysis in *Ad Beatissimi* of the divisions within society being one of the root causes of the conflict. Lack of justice and inequality between nations is what causes war and conflict. Humanity has to find a better way: 'Men nowadays are becoming more and more convinced that disputes which may arise between nations must be resolved by negotiation and agreement, and not by recourse to arms. We acknowledge that this conviction owes its origin chiefly to the terrifying destructive force of modern weapons. It arises from fear of the ghastly and catastrophic consequences of their use. Thus, in this age which boasts of its atomic power, it no longer makes sense (*alienum a ratione*) to maintain that war is a fit instrument with which to repair the violation of justice.'[67]

Just as Benedict had referred to the war as 'human madness', so nearly fifty years later John reiterated this by showing that the *nature of modern warfare* meant that it was, literally, 'foreign to reason'. This is surely the clearest development in Catholic teaching about war, moving away from a cool, theoretical reflection about how armies should behave to an assertion that war is 'out of date' because of how it has become more brutal. This teaching, which has underpinned all the subsequent calls for peace in the world by Paul VI, John Paul II and Benedict XVI, is the strongest message of *Pacem in Terris*, and we can see the lines of progression from Benedict XV's calls for peace in World War I. Similarly, just as Benedict had called for nations to look on each other in a different way, so John made it clear that disarmament would only happen if mutual fear was replaced by trust. Of course, just as

Benedict's message was rejected by national leaders during the Great War, so the subsequent message of peace from the Catholic Church has not been heeded either, with the same indications of disloyalty from local bishops and other Catholics.[68]

Condemnation of modern warfare

One of the clearest effects of this shift away from ever seeing war as acceptable has been a gradual hardening in the Church's moral evaluation of 'weapons of mass destruction', particularly nuclear weapons. Although in the 1950s Pius XII reacted with horror to the development of nuclear weapons, the hierarchies and other authorities in nuclear weapons states such as the US and Britain were reluctant to criticise national policies in this period, and even silenced those who did so.[69] This changed radically after *Pacem in Terris* and the strong condemnation of modern warfare in Vatican II's Pastoral Constitution on the Church in the Modern World, *Gaudium et Spes*[70], in December 1965. From this point ecclesiastical statements increasingly only saw the nuclear weapons as a deterrent as acceptable only as a short term measure, pending disarmament negotiations.[71] Mainstream Catholic theologians and philosophers from an early stage, seen as 'conservative' and closely aligned with the thought of John Paul II, had all along maintained that nuclear deterrent policies are wicked.[72] The natural progression of this development was that in recent years the Catholic Church has condemned nuclear weapons and nuclear deterrent theory unequivocally, in the *Compendium of the Social Doctrine of the Catholic Church*[73] and, above all, Benedict XVI's World Peace Day message for 2006, in which he wrote: 'What can be said, too, about those governments which count on nuclear arms as a means of ensuring the security of their countries? Along with countless persons of good will, one can state that this point of view is not only baneful but also completely fallacious. In a nuclear war there would be no victors, only victims.'[74] Thus we can see how Christians who demonstrate against nuclear weapons are the true heirs of Benedict XV.

Patriotism v. justice

If we ask ourselves why bishops and others in combatant states were so wary of the pope's efforts to end the war, it is clear that patriotism, simple loyalty to the state, was the principal reason. People did not want simply to *appear* to be loyal to the Kaiser or King George V; they really were. Alongside developing critique of war by Catholics and other Christians since the First World War, we have seen a questioning, particularly associated with the theological movement known as 'radical orthodoxy' of the State's increasingly absolute claims on people's loyalty, often linked to the waging of war[75]. This has led many to see the State's pretensions as inherently violent; part of why we have to question the power of the State is because western countries have so markedly moved away from faith in God, and this is part of the analysis we have seen both from Benedict and Blessed John XXIII. St Augustine taught in *The City of God* that true justice and virtue could not exist in pagan society because true worship is not offered there to the true God[76] and surely in western Europe we are in a similar situation today. Local Catholic leaders during the Great War ninety years ago genuinely believed that they still lived in basically Christian societies and that their soldiers were fighting to defend Christian values – what was disturbing to them about Benedict's analysis and his proposed solution was that challenged this picture.

As the Italian writer Carlo Falconi writes: 'It is beyond doubt that Benedict XV's message of pacifism suffered only a temporary eclipse from totalitarian warmongering. It took the horrors of the Second World War, and the inadequate conduct of Pius XII in relation to them, to cause that message to be revalued at its true worth. If, in fact, any pontificate foreshadowed and prepared the way for the miracle of John XXIII, the robust and genial Bergamasque peasant, it is that of the frail, reserved Genoese aristocrat, Giacomo della Chiesa.'[77]

Benedict's prayer for peace

Compared to his predecessor St Pius X, Benedict is not usually thought of as having an heroic degree of personal sanctity. His neat and elegant appearance (in spite of his odd physique) and a bureaucrat's mind for detail are seldom seen as attributes of this kind, and he is also known to have been short-tempered at times.[78]

His piety was deeply traditional, marked by devotion to the Sacred Heart and Our Lady; it was also *liturgical*: the devoted and recollected celebration of the Church's liturgy was enormously important to him and had a considerable effect on those around him.[79]

From the very beginning of his efforts to end the war, Benedict rooted his diplomatic moves and his public statements and letters in the spiritual life of the Catholic Church. The earliest utterances come on All Saints' Day and Christmas.

We can identify four specific initiatives of prayer.

Prayer for Peace

On 10th January 1915 he published this prayer:

'Dismayed by the horrors of a war which is bringing ruin to peoples and nations, we turn, O Jesus, to Thy most loving Heart as to our last hope. O God of Mercy, with tears we invoke Thee to end this fearful scourge. O King of Peace, we humbly implore the peace for which we long. From Thy Sacred Heart Thou did shed forth over whole world divine Charity, so that discord might end and love alone might reign among men. During thy life on earth Thy heart beat with tender compassion for the sorrows of men; in this hour made terrible with burning hate, with bloodshed and with slaughter, once more may Thy divine Heart be moved to pity. Pity the countless mothers in anguish for the fate of their sons; pity the numberless families now bereaved of their fathers; pity Europe, over which broods such havoc and disaster. Do Thou inspire rulers and peoples with counsels of meekness; do Thou heal the discords that tear the nations asunder; Thou Who didst shed They Precious Blood that they might live as brothers, bring men together once more in loving harmony. And as once before to the cry of the Apostle Peter: *Save us, Lord, we perish,* Thou didst answer with words of mercy and didst still the raging waves, so now deign to hear our trustful prayer, and give back to the world peace and tranquillity.'[80]

One of the most vivid signs of the evil wrought by war is the reaction this beautiful prayer caused in some quarters. The French government initially *forbade its public recitation*, until it was qualified in a craven reaction by the Archbishop of Paris, Cardinal Amette; one French bishop changed the pope's text, adding the words 'on conditions honourable to our Fatherland'[81]

Benedict ordered a special day of prayer for Peace to be observed throughout the world; in Europe this was to be on 7th February (Sexagesima Sunday)[82] while elsewhere it was to be on 21st March (Passion Sunday), and centred on Exposition of the Blessed Sacrament in all public and conventual churches. The form of the day of prayer was laid down, including the singing of the penitential psalm *Miserere*, recitation of the pope's prayer, litanies sung in procession and the rosary.

The 'envoys of peace'

The day after Italy entered the war, 25th May 1915, Benedict ordered Catholics all over the world to observe a fast of three days; he also asked for children to make their First Holy Communion on 30th July with the intention of ending the war. He invited children to be 'envoys of peace before the throne of God' and five thousand of them came to Rome on the day. 'In order that the record of this moment may remain graven on your minds all you lives and you may very have to remember what you heard at this fatal time from the very lips of Christ's vicar, learn from us also, my children, how for two long years men who were once innocent and affectionate like you, and are so no longer, have been tearing and killing each other…you are taking part in the most fearful expiation that God, in his hidden and infinite design, every wrought by the hands of guilty society…we have resolved to betake ourself, as to a last plank in a shipwreck, to invoking the help of God through the all-powerful means of your innocence…stretch out a hand then, dear and all powerful children, to the Vicar of Christ and strengthen his unceasing desire with your precious prayers… A single child by the splendour of his grace, moves the heart of God….'[83]

The *Incruentum Altaris*

One of the most important liturgical initiatives of his pontificate was the *Incruentum Altaris*, proclaimed on 10th August 1915, St Lawrence's day. This was an extension to priests all over the world of the privilege of being able to celebrate three Requiem Masses on All Souls Day, 2nd November. This was partly to make up for Masses not said in Chantry chapels in England and other countries which had been destroyed at the Reformation, but it was also an act of prayer for the thousands of soldiers killed already in the war: 'We perceive almost before our eyes such a multitude of men, in the flower of their age, succumb to premature death in battle; to purify their souls, though the piety of kindred be not lacking, who will say nevertheless that it is equal to the need?'[84]

Queen of Peace, Pray for us!

The Litany of Our Lady, known as the Litany of Loreto, has for centuries been at the heart of Catholic love for the Blessed Virgin. Being associated with the great shrine at Loreto, it is also particularly important in Italy. On the 5th May 1917 he added to the text of the litany the invocation *Regina Pacis, Ora pro nobis!* 'Queen of Peace, pray for us!' In May each year Catholics reflect on Mary's role as our Queen and Mother, and this focus on peace offers a powerful image. In the present-day *Collection of Masses of the Blessed Virgin Mary*[85] the Mass text of *The Blessed Virgin Mary, Queen of Peace*, draws its inspiration from this invocation. This also reflects the famous icon of 'Our Lady, Queen of Peace' in the basilica of St Mary Major in Rome, inscribed with this prayer,' Hail, most august Queen of Peace, Mother of God, through the most sacred Heart of Jesus Your Son, the Prince of Peace, procure that he may lay aside his wrath and reign over us in peace'. Benedict set up a statue of Our Lady under the same title in the basilica in 1918.[86]

Fatima 1917

Devotion to Our Lady and to the rosary was central to Benedict's life: on 18th September he wrote a letter about the rosary in relation to peace. Moreover, there occurred during his reign an event which reflects this fervent prayer, although it is not known whether he was told about it. In neutral Portugal, in the village of Fatima, there occurred from May to October 1917, at the same time as Benedict's Peace Note, a series of apparitions of the Blessed Virgin to three peasant girls. The story and message of Fatima is complex,[87] but among Our Lady's messages was an exhortation to pray the Rosary so that the war might end. We can also speculate that some of the more horrific images associated with some of the visions reflect the apocalyptic nature of twentieth century warfare. Fatima has remained associated with Christian horror of violence – after his assassination attempt on the feast of Our Lady of Fatima in 1981, Pope John Paul II, attributing his escape from death to Our Lady's prayers, had the bullet from the attempt deposited in the crown of the image at Fatima.

The monument to Benedict by Pietro Canonica in St Peter's Basilica, unveiled in 1928, depicts him in prayer, kneeling above a tomb symbolising the graves scattered throughout Europe. It is delicately decorated with olive branches and above the statue is Our Lady, presenting the infant Prince of Peace to a world in flames.

Benedict's personality and peace

It is sometimes pointed out that Benedict's peaceable personality was part of the reason why he opposed the war so strongly. The Italian writer Carlo Falconi[88] records an incident when Benedict set free a captive eagle which had been brought to him as a present, and reflects on '...his instinctive repulsion for any violent or cruel action: for him war was something terrible that should never be allowed to happen, that should be resisted at all costs, and for which one could only feel horror and the desire to suffocate and prevent it. It was as if the fact of war was in some way directly connected with his own physical weakness, the instinctive defence of a disabled being against a situation of exceptional ferocity that rendered him even more defenceless. His public and doctrinal attitude and his diplomatic action in relation to the war are all to be explained primarily by this paralysing and almost physiological horror of it.' While there is something in this, Falconi surely exaggerates these external factors: theological and religious aversion to war, for a man steeped in Christian faith, are surely more important than the fact that the pope was small and walked with a limp. It is also unfair to criticise Benedict's condemnations for not being theological enough because he did not use the traditional Just War criteria in his pronouncements: he had no time for bishops (on both sides) who sought to back the war on these grounds. For him the nature of modern warfare meant that in a sense the world had moved on; rather overstating the case, Falconi says: 'His silence did not, certainly, signify the repudiation or condemnation of all this traditional teaching, but by implication he declared it inadequate, a childish morality in an adult age, and inadequate above all because it helped to nourish rather than extinguish war.'[89]

Benedict and remembering the war dead

If we are clear about Benedict's teaching about the First World War and the influence of this teaching on how Catholic teaching about war developed in the twentieth century, and at how this vision was rooted in Catholic spirituality and liturgy, we are surely enabled to look afresh at the ways in which we remember the war dead. Benedict's *Incruentum Altaris* showed that for him, the priority was praying for the souls of dead soldiers in purgatory and offering Masses for them. How far do we follow this priority?

The reason why this is important is that all the ways in which communities join together in acts of commemoration came into being after the First World War. The imagery and symbolism is entirely taken from the conflict: the empty tomb or 'cenotaph', the bugle signals such as *The Last Post*, gun salutes, marching, the silence marking the armistice at 11am on 11th November

1918, and above all the red poppies, modelled on those from 'Flanders' Fields'. Much of this imagery has become deeply rooted in the consciousness of people all over Europe; for the majority of people in Britain who do not practice the Christian faith, this imagery is profoundly moving and does enable us not to forget the wars of the last century or those who lost their lives in them: for many such people, Remembrance Sunday ceremonies may be the only acts of worship they ever attend. It is also for many people an opportunity to make real the love they have for their Queen and country. As an observance it is also very important for Catholics who are in or have been in the armed forces, often serving in present day conflicts.

Dishonour of war

However, if we look at these ceremonies through the penetrating, bespectacled eyes of Pope Benedict XV, we surely have to conclude that much of what happens in these ceremonies is not consistent with his teaching about the war from which these commemorations sprang. Although patriotism and militarism in the ceremonies have been much reduced since the 1920s and 1930s, we are still given the impression that the deaths of World War I were noble and glorious (many a cenotaph has the inscription 'Our Glorious Dead'), and that, in the words of the Roman poet Horace, *dulce et decorum est pro patria mori* ('It is a sweet and fine thing to die for one's native land')[90]. But Benedict taught that the First World War was a 'horrible carnage that dishonours Europe' and that because of it the world had become 'a hospital and a charnel house.'

For him the conflict and what the soldiers were being made to do was devoid of nobility or grandeur: it was wrong; it should never have happened; it should have been stopped long before it did; it did not have to go on for four years; it went on for as long as it did because of the unworthy and shameful policies of the leaders of the belligerent nations.

Of course, for most people today remembering the dead of World War II, a conflict with a clearer moral compass, is what Remembrance Day is principally about, but it is surely important not to lose sight of the conflict of twenty years before that. The reason is that – partly because of Benedict XV – Catholic teaching about war and peace has developed in such a clear direction. As we saw above, since Vatican II the Church has become more and more forthright in its condemnation of war; and yet so much of the symbolism and language of Remembrance Sunday has not caught up with this. The marching, the gun salutes, the sacrilegious imposition of a sword on to the cross on so many war memorials – these are not the language of the Christian faith but of the nation states of World War I which sent millions to their deaths, demanding absolute loyalty.

Religious acts of remembrance

Worse still, some of the ways in which religious imagery was manipulated to commemorate the dead are profoundly disturbing. The hymn *O Valiant Hearts*, which is mercifully not sung much nowadays, almost blasphemously substitutes the carnage of the trenches for the sacrifice of Christ on the cross.[91] Another grotesque example is the memorial to the Machine Gun Regiment in the middle of Hyde Park Corner in London, with its inscription from 1 Samuel 18:7, 'Saul has slain his thousands, and David his tens of thousands.' We have also seen in the decades since the end of the Second World War how far states use commemorations of the war dead to build up support for their own military escapades – at present this is done every year in relation to the war in Iraq. This is at least disturbing, as Christians can never separate their commemoration of the war dead from a moral evaluation of the conflict: to deny this is to fall into the same trap as those who ignored Benedict XV or opposed him. At the very least Christians should be trying harder to improve remembrance ceremonies – and if necessary we should distance ourselves from them. The white poppy campaign, launched by the Peace Pledge Union in the 1930s was an important act of resistance to the way the British state honoured the war dead; the churches should surely be more closely identified with this; and yet, respect for the charitable work of the British Legion often prevents clergy of all churches from challenging the way in which Remembrance Sunday is celebrated.

Benedict and Versailles

The war ended with the armistice of 11th November 1918, amidst one of the consequences of the war which Benedict had most feared – the disintegration of the Austro-Hungarian empire. On 1st December he issued a very brief encyclical, *Quod Iam Diu*, full of simple rejoicing that the slaughter had ceased. Thanksgiving is due to God above all for the end of the war: 'Moved to compassion by the unceasing prayers of His servants, He now lets humanity breathe again after so many trials and sorrows.'[92] We have seen how the Holy See was not going to be allowed to the Peace Conference which convened in Versailles (nor were other neutral powers such as Spain and Holland); in spite of the some of the 'Fourteen points' of President Wilson which followed some of the calls in Benedict's Peace Note, the pope was justly fearful that the conference would be motivated not by Christian principles of reconciliation and forgiveness, but by a desire to apportion blame and exact reparations in a spirit of revenge. In the months immediately after the armistice Europe continued to suffer – through continued political instability in the Central Powers and Russia, and also as a result of the continued economic blockade and the influenza epidemic.

Some serious reservations

Much of Benedict's critique of Versailles is found in the encyclical he issued after it had finished, on 23rd May 1920, *Pacem Dei Munus*. 'This joy of our paternal heart is disturbed by many bitter anxieties, for if in most places peace is in some sort established and treaties signed, the germs of former enmities remain…there can be no stable peace…unless there be a return of mutual charity to appease hate and banish enmity.' His message was the same as it had been back in 1914 – lack of charity remained the fundamental problem. There follows a long scriptural reflection on charity; the letter also called for a 'league, or rather a sort of family' of nations[93]. Again the pope called for world-wide disarmament and European integration and unification.[94]

The Holy See had objected to the 'Guilt clause' in the Versailles Treaty, and also to the large level of reparations imposed on Germany (which it never paid anyway); it also foresaw that the disintegration of the Habsburg Empire would actually make Germany more powerful because there would be no power to balance it in central Europe. The only area where the Vatican's diplomacy was successful was in preventing the Kaiser from being brought to trial. What Versailles showed was that a peace based on victory and humiliation will always be inferior to one which results from forgiveness and compromise; no-one disputes that German humiliation at Versailles was one of the most important factors which led to the rise of Nazism in the late 1920s; nothing was done, except by the Church, to heal the wounds of the war in the years after the conference: the Ruhr crisis between France and Germany was one of the earliest signs of continuing enmity. Benedict's successor Pius XI, in his first encyclical *Ubi Arcano Dei*, published in December 1922, would be even more forthright in his criticisms, lambasting 'the spirit of bitterness and vengeance' which had been 'increased and almost given official status' by 'an artificial peace established on paper.'[95] Yet again we see Benedict's teaching and diplomacy vindicated by what actually happened.

Benedict and humanitarian relief

One of the most important and respected charities in the world is the *Save the Children Fund.* It was founded after the war in May 1919 in England by the redoubtable Eglantyne Jebb, who once said 'All wars are waged against children' and one of those who supported her from the beginning was Benedict. All the churches in England had a special collection for the charity's work on Holy Innocents' Day (28th December) 1919, and in the following year she had an audience with the pope, who also praised the charity's work in his encyclical of that year *Annus Iam Plenus.*[96] His trenchant attacks on the war were accompanied from the very beginning of the conflict by tremendous humanitarian efforts which in the end won him the grudging respect of his opponents.

Firstly he worked tirelessly to help prisoners of war. By the spring of 1915 the *Opera dei Prigionieri* had been established within the Secretariat of State, mirroring the work of the Red Cross and dealing with vast amounts of correspondence, enquiries about missing persons and help in getting sick prisoners sent home.[97] The work also extended to providing chaplains for prisoners from all faiths; also, although the practical problems were immense, he managed to arrange some prisoner exchanges and a large number of prisoners (26,000) were enabled to convalesce in neutral Switzerland. This care also extended to civilian detainees and the Holy See managed to stop deportations in Belgium.

The Vatican also launched major appeals to provide food for refugees, especially children, during and after the war years; Benedict also attempted to give protection to suffering Christians in the disintegrating Ottoman Empire – including (with little success) the Armenians, subjected to deliberate genocide at the hands of the Turks, which is why it is so ironic that the only statue ever put up in his honour (at the behest of Muslims) is in Istanbul.[98]

Financial aid

One of the many things which horrified Benedict about modern warfare was the effects on civilians of the bombardment of cities. We tend to think of this much more in relation to the Second World War (partly because by comparison little happened in Britain) but the cities of north-eastern Italy (a region in which the Della Chiesa family had an estate) – Venice, Treviso, Padua, Trieste and Pola – suffered greatly. Benedict sent considerable financial aid to the cities and tried, with only limited success, to stop the military authorities from bombing and shelling cities. How much Benedict cared about humanitarian relief for the victims of war and the famines which followed the war (including in Bolshevik Russia) is shown by the vast amount of the Vatican's money he spent on it: eighty-two million *lire*. He was generous in answering requests for help, often giving more than he was asked for. His generosity and the big drop in 'Peter's Pence' collections during the war (especially from Germany, which had been a big contributor) meant that not much was left by his death in 1922: there was so little left in the coffers that a loan had to be secured to pay for the conclave which elected Pius XI.[99] This all makes sense: generosity in the face of so much suffering is a true following of the Sermon on the Mount. In the years that followed much of Benedict's efforts were spent on continuing to help the victims of war and famine and on support for the Church's missionary work and the nurture of indigenous clergy.

Conclusion

The narrator in Anthony Burgess' epic novel *Earthly Powers*,[100] says of the year 1922, 'Pope Benedict XV, that great pacific prelate to whom neither the Germans nor the Allies would listen, Giacomo della Chiesa, James of the Church, lawyer and diplomat, hopeless with money, his prodigality of aid to the needy having put the Vatican in the red, had died…'

Illness and death

Benedict's pontificate was the shortest of the twentieth century apart from that of John Paul I, and he died at the comparatively young age of sixty-seven; he had seldom been ill, and once told Gasparri that he only ever spent one and a half *lire* on medicine for himself; but in his last years he seemed frail[101]. He caught a chill while waiting to say Mass for some sisters in the Vatican; as he had never bothered much about his health, this went to his lungs and developed into pneumonia. In spite of how he had been treated his death did lead to a great outpouring of grief in Italy, where flags flew at half mast for the first time at the death of a pope for over seventy years.

A dishonoured prophet

The brevity of his reign and the failure of his efforts during the war to broker a negotiated peace have obscured the importance of what he did, in spite of the fact that the war and its aftermath did lead greatly to an enhancement of the Holy See's place in the world, even among those not inclined to be positive, such as the governments of Italy and France, with whom relations did markedly improve – partly because he canonised Joan of Arc in 1920. In the many histories of the Great War itself he seldom receives a mention, and yet for Catholics and other Christians in our own age he is surely more important than ever. Just as prophets in the Old Testament, including many who warned against trusting in weapons of war, were dishonoured and ignored, so in his own time Benedict XV was dishonoured 'in his own country' - not only by Italy, but the family of the Catholic Church. A prophet is not primarily one who foretells the future, but one who speaks the Word of God in *truth*: and the truth about the First World War was not something which those in power in Europe wanted to face. As we seek to deepen the Church's theology of peace and help men and women to turn their backs on war and on all that glorifies war, Benedict XV is a great inspiration.[102]

Endnotes

[1] John F. Pollard, *Benedict XV The Pope of Peace* (London: Continuum 1999)

[2] D. L. O'Huallachain and J. Forrest Sharpe (eds.) *Neo-Conned! Just War Perspectives: A Condemnation of War in Iraq* (Vienna, Va.: IHS Press, 2005)

[3] '*AD REGINAM PACIS*… And to Pope Benedict XVI, with the prayerful hope that Your Holiness will vigorously defend the Church's traditional doctrine on matters of war and peace, and vindicate the rights of Truth and Justice over brute force and egotism. In doing so may Your Holiness follow in the path of Your Illustrious Predecessor, Benedict XV, whose efforts for peace were of such renown that a Muslim Committee of Paris, on behalf of all Muslims of Egypt, lamented His death with the following tribute: "…the grievous loss of His Holiness Benedict XV, that soul of an apostle of the peace of the world. If his statue set up in Constantinople, the capital of Islam, give us the consolation of making him present to us, his devout soul, his efforts for worldwide peace, his deep respect for the peoples' right to freedom will remain an undying page in the history of the whole world."'

[4] 'Filled with sentiments of awe and thanksgiving, I wish to speak of why I chose the name Benedict. Firstly, I remember Pope Benedict XV, that courageous prophet of peace, who guided the Church through turbulent times of war. In his footsteps I place my ministry in the service of reconciliation and harmony between peoples.' Pope Benedict XVI's First General Audience, 27th April 2005.

[5] Quoted in Pollard, op. cit. p.13

[6] See Pollard, op. cit., pp. 24ff., who warns against a simplistic analysis of what happened.

[7] *Ibid*., pp. 35ff.

[8] The first ballots were on 1st September. It may not seem rushed to us, but it should be remembered that most of the North American cardinals were not able to get to Rome before the *end* of the conclave (Pollard pp. 59ff.)

[9] *Ibid*., p.59.

[10] *Ibid*., p.67.

[11] W. H Peters, *The Life of Benedict XV* (Milwaukee:Bruce, 1959), p.88

[12] *Acta Apostolicae Sedis* 6 (1914), pp.501ff.

[13] For Benedict, this is a reference to nationalism rather than what we understand as racism.

[14] Peters, op. cit., pp.111ff; AAS 6 (1914), pp. 565ff.

[15] The film *Joyeux Noêl* (2004) and the book by M. Brown and S. Seaton, *Christmas Truce* (London: Pan, 2001).

[16] H. Johnson, *Vatican Diplomacy in the World War* (Oxford, 1933)

[17] In 1908 Asquith had played a big part in stopping a proposed pubic Procession of the Host near Westminster Cathedral for the International Eucharistic Congress; he had an icy meeting with the pope during a visit to Rome in 1916 (Roy Jenkins, *Asquith* [London: Collins, 1964], pp.189ff. and 391). '"His aversion from the Roman Catholic faith was dour and inveterate" wrote Winston Churchill of the Conservative leader Arthur Balfour. Of Asquith, Balfour's Liberal rival, it is said

that he had two lifelong aversions, eating rabbit, and the Roman Catholic Church.' (A. Hastings, *A History of English Christianity 1920-1985* [London: Collins, 1986], p.131, quoting Churchill's *Great Contemporaries*).

[18] Britain did send a minister as special representative at the beginning of the war, Sir Henry Howard, succeeded in 1916 by Count John de Salis (A. Randall, *Vatican Assignment* [London: Heinemann, 1956], p.12), but the representation did not achieve the status of a full diplomatic legation until after the war. There was no corresponding representation of the Holy See in London.

[19] As Pollard points out (p.95) the Germans argued that Belgium had effectively violated its own neutrality by making contact with the French High Command before the war, and that Belgian civilians had fired on German soldiers; later in the war it is clear that the British and French violated the neutrality of Greece, and the Vatican had large dossiers detailing atrocities committed by all sides.

[20] Allocution to consistory, 22nd January 1915, AAS 7 (1915), pp.33ff.

[21] Note to the Belgian government, quoted in Peters, op. cit., p.121.

[22] See H. Hardach, *The First World War, 1914-1918* (London, 1977), p.37, who points out that although both actions are illegal there is a marked difference of degree between confiscating goods and sinking a ship without warning, with its crew and passengers on board.

[23] Pollard op. cit. p.122, who points out that strictly speaking Benedict was not correct.

[24] Pollard p.122, quoting D. R. Zivojinovic, *The United States and the Vatican Policies* (Boulder, Co.: 1978), an author who has tried to show that Benedict and Gasparri were not neutral at all but far more sympathetic to Germany and Austria – Hungary than is usually admitted.

[25] Johnson, op. cit., p.18. Pollard thinks that Benedict, like many in the Vatican, was paranoid about Freemasonry.

[26] See Peter Hebblethwaite, *John XXIII The Pope of the Council* (London: Chapman, 1984), pp. 80ff., and Josephine Robinson, *John XXIII Universal Parish Priest* (London: CTS B 692)

[27] C. Seton Watson, *Italy from Liberalism to Fascism* (London, 1967), p.479.

[28] Pollard, op. cit. pp.129-130, who does not refer to the accounts of Benedict's popularity among retreating soldiers, and stresses that, particularly after the situation had stabilised, both he and clergy and bishops near the front line were criticised for defeatism, in spite of practical efforts which were made by the Church to help suffering civilians. The pope was also blamed by *The Times* of London for Italian lack of resistance, part of the constant thread of British anti-Catholicism; worse still was the *Morning Post*.

[29] J. Derek Holmes, *The Papacy in the Modern World 1914-1978* (London: Burns and Oates, 1981), p.6; AAS 7 (1915), pp.365ff.

[30] Pollard, op. cit., p.118.

[31] *Ibid*., pp.118-119.

[32] Holmes, op. cit., p.6.

[33] He was beatified by Pope John Paul II in 2004.

[34] Pollard, op. cit. pp.119-120 and Peters, op. cit. p.141. As far as Benedict was concerned there was little point in antagonising the Entente powers if the German initiative had nothing substantial to offer. The Vatican's approach did lead to a coolness in relations with Germany in the first half of 1917.

[35] 'The President is not proposing peace; he is not even offering mediation. He is merely proposing that soundings be taken in order that we may learn, the neutral nations with the belligerents, how hear the haven of peace may be for which all mankind longs with an intense and increasing longing', Pollard, op. cit., pp.120-121.

[36] He was surely in a position to broker a peace, far more so than the pope. As A. J. P. Taylor says, 'It was ironical that he abandoned neutrality just when his mediation might have achieved some purpose at last.' (*From Sarajevo to Potsdam* [London, 1966], p.42)

[37] Pollard, op. cit., p.123.

[38] Holmes, op. cit., p 11; AAS 9 (1917), pp. 417ff.

[39] H. E. G. Rope, *Benedict XV The Pope of Peace* (London: Gifford, 1941), p.132.

[40] Youssef Tanouk, *The Roman Catholic Church in Britain during the First World War: A Study in Political Leadership* (Doctoral thesis, University of Western Sydney, 2003; available online at library.uws.edu.au/adt-NUWS/uploads/approved/adt-NWS20040701.164.232), pp.273ff., refers to efforts to challenge the government's desultory response. Asquith had by now been replaced by Lloyd George, but the Foreign Secretary Arthur Balfour was just as anti-Catholic (see note 19 above).

[41] Op. cit. p.151. According to Taylor (op. cit., p. 43) Wilson, a strict Calvinist, was anti-Catholic.

[42] The others included open diplomacy, the creation of the League of Nations, the restoration of Belgium, independence for Poland, proper frontiers for Italy (challenging the Treaty of London), an ambiguous solution for Alsace-Lorraine, and autonomy for the peoples of Austria-Hungary and the Ottoman Empire (D. Stevenson, *1914-1918 The History of the First World War* [London: Penguin, 2004], pp. 391-392).

[43] Quoted in Pollard, op. cit., p.128.

[44] Quoted in Holmes, op. cit., p.12.

[45] E. Oldmeadow, *Francis Cardinal Bourne*, Volume II (London: Burns and Oates, 1940-1944), p.116. Bourne had been in Rome at the time of the German Peace Note in December 1916. He denounced it to Italian journalists as 'a piece of common trickery' and 'a vulgar trap'. He wrote to the Duke of Norfolk assuring him that he was doing his best in Rome to serve the Allies' cause, and that 'Italian opinion, especially in clerical circles, is somewhat lukewarm, and too ready for peace at any price.' (*Ibid.*, p. 115). Bourne went to the trenches to bless the troops, and joined Admiral Jellicoe with the Grand Fleet after the Battle of Jutland; he had a long track record of encouraging young men to fight for their country (*Ibid.*, the whole of chapter XIV, pp. 106ff.) Oldmeadow does not mention the Pope's Peace Note or any of his specific initiatives, let alone the Guild.

[46] Tanouk, op. cit., pp. 231ff. The 'Preliminary Notice' quoted *Allorchè Fummo* and also stated that the Guild's aim was 'to help now towards the making of the Pope's Peace. For the achievement of this end the Guild will press for the Holy Father's own

suggested methods – methods which, indeed, he calls "the only way"'. These were 1) a truce; 2) a declaration of conciliatory peace terms, and 3) an immediate conference. 'Only the Pope's Peace, a spiritual peace, can be either holy or permanent, for any other will be founded on militarism, vengeance, force, and worldly ambitions.'

[47] Bishop Amigo wrote: 'While realising the purity of the sentiments of Catholic devotion and loyalty to the Holy See, which animate the promoters of such a Guild, I think that this notice, considering the temper of the country at the present time, is like to arouse the gravest misunderstandings, and I am sorry that it seem to come out with the approval of the authorities of this diocese when I have not been consulted. I am sure that you will agree with me in regretting it being issued.' (M. Clifton: *Amigo Friend of the Poor* [Leominster: Fowler Wright, 1987] p.56) Amigo had played a part in discouraging Spain from joining the war on Germany's side.

[48] Complied by E. I Watkin (London, 1916). Tanouk, op. cit., pp.236ff., gives details of the passionately argued correspondence in *The Universe* between leading members of the Guild and their critics. The only bishop who was in any way sympathetic to the Guild was the Bishop of Northampton, Frederick Keating (subsequently Archbishop of Liverpool) and as note 58 below shows even his support for the pope was distinctly lukewarm.

[49] *Catholic Times* 28th April 1916.

[50] Reprinted in *The Universe* 15th September 1916.

[51] Quoted in A. Rhodes, *The Power of Rome in the Twentieth Century* (New York: F. Watts, 1983), p.242.

[52] Tanouk, op. cit., pp.257-258.

[53] Quoted in Rhodes, op. cit., p.242. Bourne's position mirrored that of the established Church of England, particularly in Anglican papers such as the *Church Quarterly Review*. He co-operated with Archbishop Randall Davidson in backing the King's call in October 1914 for abstinence from alcohol for the duration of the war (G. K. A. Bell, *Randall Davidson* [Oxford, 1938], pp. 748-749).

[54] '[The Guild's] belief border on heresy; its objects are indistinguishable from those of the 'stop-the-war' organisations already in existence...[it is] an essentially anti-patriotic society..' The paper objected to a 'few laymen' (overlooking the involvement of clergy on the committee) who presumed to act on the pope's wishes. Rather, 'If concerted action on the lines of the Guild...were necessary...we may be sure that the Bishops, who...are more likely to be safe interpreters of the Pope's intentions...would have taken the appropriate steps', *The Universe*, 12th May 1917. This sycophantic and misleading nonsense of course reflects the attitude prevalent at the time towards laypeople.

[55] 15th December 1916, after the German peace offer.

[56] Tanouk writes: '*The Tablet*, for example, while approving some of the terms proposed by the Pope, rejected the Note in no uncertain terms. It argued that moral justice was alien to the German ideal of *Kultur*. The Tablet conceded that if Belgian redemption could not be restored by the sword "then there is much to say for the poor second-best which would secure the restoration of her territory by a promise to let bygones be bygones." It was only fair, *The Tablet* continued, that the Peace Note be judged on the assumption that the Allies could not attain

complete victory. But such an assumption, the paper added, was not shared by the British "and certainly not by anyone connected with this journal."' (op. cit., p. 251, quoting *The Tablet*, 18th August 1917)

[57] Tanouk, op. cit., p. 261.

[58] So Bishop Casartelli criticised the tone of the *Manchester Guardian's* attacks but wrote that 'it is quite open for us, even for Catholics, to maintain that the Pope's proposals are inadequate, or unacceptable as being too favourable to our adversaries.' Bishop Keating in a sermon made clear the distinction between doctrinal and diplomatic documents and said 'An English Catholic…was free to form his own opinion without any violation of his obedience' although he did concede that 'no English Catholic worthy of the name was free to forget that the utterance of the Father of Christendom', in image which recalls the French professor referred to in note 44 above. (*Ibid*., pp. 258-259). Bourne also defended the pope in the face of attacks against him in the *Morning Post* after Caporetto (Oldmeadow, op. cit., pp.110-111).

[59] With regard to the famous letter of Lord Lansdowne written later in 1917 (Tanouk, op. cit., p.271); he had also been very belligerent in 1915 (*Ibid*., p.225). He went to Rome to see the Pope and try to counteract what he saw as excessive German influence.

[60] *Pope Benedict's Note to the Belligerents* (Bristol: J. W. Arrowsmith, 1917)

[61] London: Catholic Social Guild, 1917 and 1918 respectively. Earlier in the war the *St Francis' Magazine*, the magazine of the diocese of Northampton, had been one of the few Catholic publications to be positive about a negotiated peace. There are also three important articles in the Jesuit periodical *The Month* written during the war by S. F. Smith supporting the pope's efforts.

[62] On Catholic outrage at the exclusion, the deception about it and refusals to change the clause, see Tanouk, op. cit., pp.264ff. The existence of the clause was made public by the Bolsheviks after the second Russian Revolution; considerable confusion was caused by a mistranslation of the text in the *Manchester Guardian* which led some Catholics to think that the Entente powers were not simply bound to exclude the Holy See from any peace conference, but also to oppose any of its diplomatic moves towards peace.

[63] 'There was no doubt in Stein's mind…or indeed in that of any of the professoriate or students at Gottingen…that Germany had engaged in a war that was at once both just and unavoidable. Like so many others, they believed that the values at stake were those of *Kultur*, values threatened by French cynicism, British commercial self-seeking, and Russian barbarism.' (A. MacIntyre, *Edith Stein A Philosophical Prologue* [London: Continuum 2006], p.69)

[64] See E. Tolansky and H. Scott, *Pius XII* (London: CTS, B 674)

[65] London: CTS S 264. See Hebblethwaite, op. cit., chapter 23, 'Last Will and Testament.'

[66] Hebblethwaite records that John was painfully aware how in his last months he was systematically undermined by curial officials who expected to be loyal to him, specifically in relation to his work for peace – men who were taking advantage of the fact that he was dying of cancer. This recalls the disloyalty which Benedict encountered.

[67] 126-127.

[68] Examples would include Pope Paul VI's opposition to the Vietnam War and his clashes with President Lyndon Johnson (who was supported by Cardinal Francis Spellman and many of the American bishops; see on this P. Hebblethwaite, *Paul VI The First Modern Pope* [London: HarperCollins 1993,], chapter 29) and John Paul II's opposition to both Gulf wars; on dissent from this teaching see O'Huallachain and Forrest Sharpe, op.cit.

[69] As happened with Thomas Merton, at the hands of the Cistercian authorities, in the early 1960s.

[70] Paragraph 80: 'The Council, endorsing the condemnations of total warfare issued by recent popes, declares: Every act of war directed to the indiscriminate destruction of whole cities or vast areas with their inhabitants is a crime against God and man, which merits firm and unequivocal condemnation.'

[71] Pope John Paul II at the United Nations Special Session on Disarmament, 11th June 1982 (AAS 74[1982], 879).

[72] See W. Stein (ed.) *Nuclear Weapons and Christian Conscience* (London: Methuen, 1961), especially the essays by Elizabeth Anscombe and Peter Geach, and J. Finnis, J. Boyle and G. Grisez, *Nuclear Deterrence, Morality and Realism* (Oxford, 1987).

[73] English ed., London: Continuum, 2005, paragraph 508: '…The Magisterium has made a moral evaluation of the phenomenon of *deterrence*." The *accumulation of arms* strikes many as a paradoxically suitable way of deterring potential adversaries from war. They see it as the most effective way of ensuring peace among nations. This method of deterrence gives rise to strong moral reservations. The *arms race* does not ensure peace. Far from eliminating the causes of war, it risks aggravating them." Policies of nuclear deterrence, typical of the Cold War period, must be replaced with concrete measures of disarmament based on dialogue and multilateral negotiations.'

[74] http://www.vatican.va/holy_father/benedict_xvi/messages/peace/documents/hf_be-xv1_mes_20051213_xxxix-world-day-peace_en.html. The hierarchies of Scotland and of England and Wales have opposed the government's plans to renew the Trident programme: we have come a long way from the days of Cardinal Bourne.

[75] See, for example, W. Cavanaugh, *Torture and Eucharist* (Oxford: Blackwell, 1999) and J. Milbank *Theology and Social Theory* (2nd ed., Oxford: Blackwell, 2006)

[76] 19.24.

[77] C. Falconi, *The Popes in the Twentieth Century*, tr. M. Grindrod (London: Weidenfield and Nicolson, 1967) p.150.

[78] See, for example, Peters' account of the incident with Jacchini his coach driver (pp.219-220).

[79] Peters (op. cit., pp. 220-221) records a bishop's picture of the pope celebrating a Requiem Mass for his predecessor St Pius X: '…Benedict XV, walking slowly around the catafalque with censor in hand, eyes closed, lips moving, as with great deliberation he recited the *Pater Noster* in silence…the thought struck him that Christ would have performed this ceremony in precisely the same manner. He recalls how awed he was and how happy to be a priest, an instrument of the Mystical Christ.'

[80] Holmes, op. cit., p.5.

[81] Peters, op. cit., p.124.

[82] This was the name given to the second Sunday before Lent in the calendar used before the revision of 1969. Passion Sunday was the Fifth Sunday of Lent, not (as now) Palm Sunday.

[83] Rope, op. cit., pp.104-105.

[84] Quoted in Peters, op. cit., pp.237-238. The text of the bull (in Italian) can be found at http://www.vatican.va/holy_father/benedict_xv/bulls/documents/hf_ben-xv_bulls_19150.

[85] English translation, Collegeville, Minnesota: Liturgical Press, 1992. This is part of the text of proper preface for this Mass:

'…She is your lowly handmaid, receiving your word from the angel Gabriel
And conceiving in her virginal womb the Prince of Peace, Jesus Christ, Your Son, Our Lord.
She is the faithful mother, standing fearless beside the cross
As her Son sheds his blood for our salvation and reconciles all things to himself in peace.
She is the disciple of Christ and daughter of peace, joining in prayer with the apostles
As she awaits your promised gift, the Spirit of unity and peace, of love and joy…' (p.161)

[86] Rope, op. cit., pp.106-107.

[87] See the declaration of the Sacred Congregation for the Doctrine of the Faith, *The Message of Fatima*, 26th June 2006, http://www.vatican.va/roman_curia /congregations/cfaith/documents/rc_con_cfaith_doc_20000626_message_fatima which also includes John Paul II's Prayer for peace based on the apparitions, and Leo Madigan, *What Happened at Fatima* (CTS, D651). The text of one of the secrets includes these words: 'The war is going to end: but if people do not stop offending God, a worse one will break out during the pontificate of Pius XI'.

[88] Op. cit., p.115ff.

[89] *Ibid*. p.118.

[90] *Odes* 3.2.13. Although the disappearance of Latin from the school curriculum is a calamity, fortunately today many schoolchildren are taught about the great War poets, and thus may be familiar with Wilfred Owen's pastiche of this written in 1917, '*Dulce et Decorum Est,*' where he calls the phrase and the sentiment 'that old lie.'

[91] It was written by J. S Arkwright, in *Songs of Praise* [Oxford, rev. ed., 1932] hymn 293.

[92] AAS 10 (1918), pp. 473ff.

[93] AAS 12 (1920), pp. 209ff. The Holy See was of course excluded from the League of Nations; initially Germany was as well, and the United States refused to join. The conciliatory tone of the encyclical contrasts with the attitude of Cardinal Bourne, who said just after the armistice: 'An enormous debt of justice has accumulated against our enemies – a debt which the justice of God requires them to pay to those whom they have injured so deeply.' (Oldmeadow, op. cit., p. 116)

[94] Pollard, op. cit., p. 147, quoting P. Mizzi, *L'Unione Europea nei documenti pontifici* (Malta, 1979)

[95] Holmes, op. cit., p.21.

[96] 1st December 1920, AAS 12 (1920), pp. 553ff.

[97] Pollard, op. cit., p.113.

[98] Rope, op. cit., p.6, remarks:'… Signore Aristide Arstorio wrote in the *Giornale d'Italia*: "May an anti-clerical of longstanding be permitted to express an opinion regarding the late Pontiff? Benedict is a saint!" Such a tribute is indeed eloquent. In Moslem Stamboul a monument was raised by Moslem authority to this Christian hero, while among ourselves birth-preventers are shamefully honoured.'

[99] Holmes, op. cit., p.18.

[100] Harmondsworth: Penguin, 1981, p.199.

[101] See Randall, op. cit., p.1, who describes his frailty when he met him in 1920.

[102] Rope ends his biography with this tribute in verse:

'Sole voice of peace amid the raging sea
Of hate and slaughter, cries and countercries
Of stricken, bought and sold humanity,
Sole voice of truth amid the storm of lies.

Sole voice of love amid the roar of hate
That sunders race from race and man from man,
When all the thoughtless world is desolate
Sole king and seer the Law of God to scan.

His Law thou meditating day and night
Unto a blind bewilder'd world dost speak,
Unwearied, swerving never left or right,
Blessing, and blest, rock-steadfast, valiant, meek.'